Eastern Steam Days Remembered II

Think this is 1st copy

STANDARDS REMOVED

Strathwood

Eastern Steam Days Remembered II

Front Cover: Top Shed at Kings Cross demonstrates why it was known as such with the presentation of their own 60034 Lord Farringdon, alongside 60143 Sir Walter Scott from 52A Gateshead and 60522 Straight Deal off 50A York in this superb shot from around 1960 at Kings Cross. *Colour Rail*

Strathwood

Eastern Steam Days Remembered II

A selection of some of the essential books and magazines from the era along with a few other reminders of the locomotives.

First published 2019

ISBN 978-1-913390-03-7

Copyright Strathwood Publishing 2019
Published by Strathwood Publishing, 9 Boswell Crescent, Inverness, IV2 3ET
Telephone 01463 234004
Printed by Akcent Media

Contents

Preface

I have grabbed the opportunity once again to ask my old friend Roger Stanton to draft up some more of his memories involving Eastern Region steam to open this second volume on the subject.

As a result of being a child from the late 1950s, my own recollections of Eastern and North Eastern Region steam are very much limited to one journey from Kings Cross to Newcastle when visiting relations in Ashington in the early 1960s accompanied by my mother. I recall looking out the window for just about the entire journey, thrilled by everything I saw.

Subsequent visits to Ashington were always made in my father's car sadly. But as my aunt and uncle lived less than thirty yards from a signal box protecting a level crossing, everyone knew where to find me,

watching the J27s, K1s and Ivatt Class 4MT working their local coal trains.

We will all have our favourites from the past, I hope you will enjoy this compilation and we must also thank the foresight of the photographers and the kindness of those who have allowed their work to be seen and appreciated by a wider audience too.

Kevin Derrick
Inverness 2019

Below: A little before my time in 1952, this was the everyday scene for all of the lads spotting on the platforms at Doncaster, as Gresley A3 60091 Captain Cuttle speeds through with an up express. *Colour Rail*

Introduction -
My Eastern Steam
Days Remembered

Well yes, they are and always will be!

To me the Eastern Region of British Railways was anywhere that you could find locomotives whose number started with a 6! Obviously Included in this heading was also the Great Eastern, North Eastern and Scottish Region's lines of British Railways. This album will recall those days with nostalgia.

Geographically the overall region was vast covering something like a third of the United Kingdom from Kings Cross and the London suburbs to East Anglia and the Fens with large swathes of the East Midlands. Heading north much of Yorkshire and the North East was eastern territory before heading into Scotland where lines spread far and wide from Edinburgh to Fife to Wick and Thurso and west to Mallaig. The region also crossed the Pennines to Manchester, Chester and just into North Wales.

Naturally there was a huge range of motive power and services to be observed from express passenger traffic to coal and many other types of freight to a plethora of country branch lines that led a bucolic life that many of us thought would last forever! Many of the locomotives were also unique to the area where they worked owing to their original heritage and would normally never be seen elsewhere. There were exceptions to this, of course with a good example being the allocation of Holden's B12, F4, J67 & J69 locomotives of Great Eastern parentage being sent to the North East of Scotland and working from depots such as Keith and Aberdeen Kittybrewster.

My own first interest in eastern steam and railways started with one of those meandering minor lines although from what I've read over the

Above: Setting off with a local from St. Olaves in September 1958, was Gresley Class B17 Sandringham, 61656 Leeds United with an easy load for this 4-6-0. *Colour Rail*

years the staff that served on this railway did not consider themselves a minor railway at all!

I was born in Holbeach on the Midland and Great Northern Joint Railway which ran from a junction just east of Nottingham at Saxby eventually running all the way to Great Yarmouth with branches to Peterborough, Cromer and Norwich. My father built a house in Cranmore Lane only fifty yards from the line so it should come as no surprise that myself and several friends spent a fair bit of time at the minor crossing waiting for and watching the trains that passed. I had been told by my parents to watch out for the Royal Train as it may come that way taking the King to his residence at Sandringham. I never saw it, though!

Obviously, I was far too young to know what I was looking at but I suspect that most of the locomotives were Gresley's Class J6 of which several

occupied by the railway was now a huge car park giving an indication of how large the railway facility once was.

Other memories of the Spalding and Holbeach area are of seeing an almost brand-new 61379 Mayflower on the morning express from Cleethorpes to Kings Cross. My grandmother was on the train and we made a special journey to Spalding to see her during the short stop. Another unforgettable memory was the sight of 61657 Doncaster Rovers of 31B March shed in absolutely sparkling condition heading non-stop through Spalding. Little did I know that within two or three years she would be gone for scrap.

A family move was made at this time and I found myself living in Grimsby. Due to the circumstances I was not sent immediately to school and quickly developed a wanderlust which took me to Cleethorpes and the sea front. We also had a local station at New Clee only a few yards away from where I lived along with vast marshalling yards for the fish traffic as Grimsby was recognised as the largest fishing port in the world at that time. This of course meant lots and lots of new trains to watch! The footbridge at Fuller Street was a great observation point as you could see all the excursion traffic that laid up there during the day before heading back to all points west such as Sheffield, Rotherham and other industrial centres that sent excursions to Cleethorpes all summer long. I soon found out what Thompson's Class B1s were as they would be common traction for much of the traffic. Most were local examples from Immingham, Lincoln or Sheffield Darnall but there was the occasional K3 or even a K2 to spice up the spotting. In the fish sidings J94 tanks pottered about daily marshalling the trains that would leave to what seemed to be all parts of the country. Oddities such as the occasional Midland Crab 2-6-0 would also appear from time to time.

were allocated to 40F Boston and 35A New England (Peterborough). Some of the New England locomotives would probably be working from the sub-shed at Spalding. I do remember that every afternoon on our way home from primary school we would pass a large black freight engine parked just west of Holbeach Station which I now identify as a Class J39, a type also common in the area. The Ivatt 4MTs had not appeared by the time the family left to go and live in Grimsby but were noted later during visits to friends in the area.

I can remember the family used the M&GN quite regularly for shopping trips into Spalding and day trips to places like Hunstanton, which my memories tell me was a very busy place in the summer with holiday traffic. On my last trip to Hunstanton some years ago the entire area

Then just as I was appreciating the local scene another family move was made. This time to a part of the country that I thought was not eastern territory! We were going to live in Rugby in Warwickshire with my other grandparents and I was introduced to the London Midland Region with a vengeance. My world was now re-built Royal Scots, Patriots, Jubilees, Coronation Pacifics and so on. But one day when out with friends I stumbled across a railway line that previously I had no idea of it's very existence. It was not long before a freight appeared heading south with great gusto and the locomotive carried a number starting with a 6! I later discovered that it was a Thompson O1 being rebuilt from an original Robinson O4. It wasn't alone either as presently another appeared followed by yet another. I'd discovered the Great Central! Yet another company subsumed into the London North Eastern Railway at grouping in 1923 and now part of the Eastern Region of British Railways.

Before long I had discovered the now dismantled Abbey Street girder bridge where we could observe both the Eastern and London Midland Region's lines along with, at times it seemed up to a thousand other like-minded youngsters during the summer holidays. It was a perfect spot with Adderley's corner shop in Winfield Street and a nearby chip shop about a hundred yards away in Abbey Street. All bases covered as they say!

I soon discovered that the Great Central offered a wide range of motive power. We were still able to enjoy a Robinson Class A5 4-6-2 tank from 38A Colwick (Nottingham) shed on the morning local and Gresley's A3 Pacifics were largely still in charge of the express passenger traffic plus a whole range of other ex-LNER types. Along with all this we also had a daily visit from a Great Western locomotive once a day on the Inter-regional Bournemouth – York express.

Although, to me the Eastern Region of British Railways started at Kings Cross in North London. I was lucky enough to have an aunt who lived near Borough on the Northern Line of the London Underground so it was an easy step to jump on the tube and a few stops later you were at Kings Cross. The range of passenger locomotives to be seen was varied with examples of the A1/2/3 and A4 Pacifics all to be seen daily along with the suburban N2 0-6-2 tanks until they were replaced by the Diesel Multiple Units and a few other types such as B1s and B17s on outer suburban and Cambridge line traffic. The main Kings Cross motive power depot was hidden away amongst the extensive goods yards, but I was lucky enough to make one visit before the end of steam.

Seventy-odd miles north of London is the cathedral city of Peterborough which I was again lucky enough to visit a few times for spotting trips. This being the nearest point of access from Rugby. I only remember a couple of trips on the east coast mainline and heading north we always turned east at Werrington Junction for Spalding or Grimsby. A journey now sadly no longer possible via the long-closed East Lincolnshire line via Boston.

My next contact with Eastern Region steam came in the Doncaster and Sheffield area as family trips now used the Great Central line to Sheffield and thence to Grimsby with a choice of routes from there onwards either by Gainsborough or Scunthorpe. Both suited me as there was always something of interest to see! My first trip via Sheffield and the Great Central was noteworthy for the appearance of Gresley

Left: A gaggle of schoolboys in their brown blazers are on hand to greet the arrival of a Gresley Sandringham, 61654 Sunderland into Melton Constable during 1956.
Colour Rail

A3 Pacific 60054 Prince of Wales which was to take us as far as Leicester where it would be exchanged for something else for the run up to London Marylebone.

At this time, of course the coal industry was still huge, and freight would be observed just about everywhere with many different types of freight locomotives. Much of this traffic emanated from the East Midlands around Nottingham heading for London and much was routed away from the Great Northern mainline on to the Great Northern and Eastern Joint line via March and the huge Whitemoor marshalling yard. March had it's own locomotive depot coded 31B which I visited just the once. This was right at the end of steam and several strangers were on shed including a London Midland Region Patriot 4-6-0 from 2B Nuneaton shed.

All the Eastern Region sheds in the Sheffield area were also visited as part of a coach trip sometime back in 1962. These included 41A Sheffield, 41H Staveley (GC), 41J Langwith Junction, 41F Mexborough and the two depots at Retford 36E. Retford was unusual as there was an ex Great Northern depot servicing the east coast route and a much larger ex-GC depot nearby. If you visited these depots at a weekend you would see whole lines of freight locomotives lined up awaiting fresh work on the Monday morning.

Sadly, I never got to see the Eastern Region north of Doncaster but there was a huge amount of interest for the enthusiast. My one trip to Hull was work related with a new job and I was just in time to see the depot at Dairycoates with lines of withdrawn locomotives. It was 1966 and the end was very near, but the local depot still rostered a Thompson B1 on it's portion of the Yorkshire Pullman for a few more weeks. The other depots at Springhead and Botanic Gardens had long since closed as Yorkshire had been the "test bed" for diesel multiple units since the mid-1950s replacing all the local steam operated passenger services.

From York northwards the Eastern Region had an amazing amount of interest with a tangle of lines to Scarborough in the east and back again towards Leeds, Harrogate and Bradford in the west and on to Darlington in the North. Strangely Leeds had a small representation by the Eastern Region with just one small locomotive depot at 37A/56C Copley Hill. I note both codes as I was at Peterborough one day when an A1 Pacific rolled in bearing the code 56C on it's smokebox. This code did not appear in my shed book and thus caused much confusion among the gathered enthusiasts. It was only explained something like three months later when Trains Illustrated revealed the regional changes that had taken place. Ardsley 37B/56B was the freight depot nearest to Leeds being in the middle of nowhere halfway between Leeds and Wakefield. If you go there today it is almost impossible to believe that it and it's accompanying marshalling yard ever existed! The major eastern shed in Bradford at Hammerton St went the same way as the Hull depots as part of the DMU revolution and was converted to a diesel maintenance depot but only lasted a few years before closure. One side effect of this was the transfer of most remaining eastern locomotive power to 56F Low Moor which was the ex-Lancashire and Yorkshire shed.

The north-east around Darlington, Sunderland and Newcastle was an absolute hot bed of steam. Heavy

Left: Legendary ECML driver Bill Hoole stands proudly in front of 60007 Sir Nigel Gresley alongside the shed at Doncaster on 23 May 1959, while his steed for the day is being prepared for the Stephenson Jubilee Railtour. *Colour Rail*

Flying the flag once again for the cleaners and the railwaymen based out of 34A Kings Cross in October 1961, was 60008 Dwight D. Eisenhower as this magnificent Gresley Pacific edges back under the coaling tower for one last top-up before setting off for the day. *Colour Rail*

Shed Bash South

One of the condenser fitted Class N2s from Gresley, 69538 is flanked by a pair of Thompson's Class L1s, 67793 and 67749 outside the 'Met' shed at Kings Cross during October 1960. Signs of what is to come lurk to the right-hand side with an English Electric Type 4 and B.T.H. Type 1. *Rail Photoprints*

Opposite: Burnished to absolute perfection and a testament to the Top Shed staff as 60003 Andrew K. McCosh stands ready for service this morning outside 34A Kings Cross. *Roy Edgar Vincent/The Transport Treasury*

Opposite: No way near as much glitter but still more respectable than many a 52A Gateshead allocated Gresley A4 Pacific, the condition of 60008 Dwight D. Eisenhower when seen on 5 August 1962, has slipped somewhat in service since our first view of the locomotive. *Colour Rail*

The shed code for Peterborough's New England shed changed from 35A to 34E during July 1958. The shed plate worn by 60025 Falcon reflects this when it was seen here during June 1963, having just been transferred here from Top Shed to eke out its last four months in service. *Colour Rail*

Opposite: Also beneath the overhead watering gantry at New England a few years earlier on 10 April 1960, the reasonably clean Class A2/3 60500, was named after its designer Edward Thompson and awaits further developments. *Colour Rail*

The externally rundown condition of another of Thompson's Class A2/3s at New England on 16 May 1963, reflects the fact that 60520 Owen Tudor was withdrawn exactly one month later. *Colour Rail*

When photographed at Grantham in May 1958, DMUs were already threatening the efforts of this Class A5, 69814 to find regular local passenger work from its home shed here. With the tender full of coal the fireman onboard Gresley Class A3, 60047 Donovan, is busy making up his fire judging from the black smoke emitted from the double chimney on this visit to 34F Grantham in July 1961, this was five months before the locomotive gained its smoke deflectors. *Both: Colour Rail*

Taking a trip around the shed's unusual turning triangle here at Grantham, the world-famous 60022 Mallard gives us a quick pop from its chime whistle as they make their way around to turn, with the shed buildings in the background in May 1962. *Colour Rail*

Another 2-8-0 built by North British in Glasgow to a war department contract was 90189, which is also seen on shed at Retford. Although 90189 was not built until August 1943, it was no doubt thanks to being rebuilt in 1944, 63785 seen on the previous page gave twenty-six more years of active service to the nation's railways, far more than 90189 would ever be allowed to. Doncaster shed plays host to Gresley's pioneer Class V2, 60800 Green Arrow. When it was introduced in June 1936 it was the first three-cylinder 2-6-2 locomotive to run on Britain's railways. Designed for fast mixed traffic

work, the LNER's publicity department seized the chance to have the locomotive named Green Arrow which was their marketing name for the LNER's new special fast freight service. With the construction of the one hundred and eighty-four V2s carrying on through into 1944, it has often been said that these really were the engines that won the war, by helping to keep the massively increased traffic along the ECML moving through to long war years. *Both: Colour Rail*

Opposite: It's a very different colour being celebrated on shed at 36A Doncaster on 9 June 1963, as the shed sees the arrival of lots of spotters brought to South Yorkshire from Kings Cross onboard the Home Counties Railway Society's special headed by Stanier's Duchess Pacific 46245 City of London. Having cleaned her fire and taken coal, the pride of the rival WCML takes it easy for the afternoon as the tour's participants also visited the works. *John Rowe*

We also make a visit to Doncaster Works over a lunch break three days beforehand to find the partly dismembered remains of Gresley Class A3, 60056 Centenary. Built here in February 1925, we can see she didn't live up to what her nameplates still proclaimed as she was being broken up on 6 June 1963, after thirty-eight years of service along the southern reaches of the ECML. *Colour Rail*

Simmering nicely on her home shed here at Doncaster on 19 July 1959, was 60125 Scottish Union. One of the Class A1 Pacifics introduced during Peppercorn's reign as CME in April 1949. Sadly also being shortlived she would go for scrap herself to Cox & Danks at Wadsley Bridge in the Autumn of 1964. *Colour Rail*

Opposite: All is well on the footplate of this double chimney fitted Class A3, 60093 Coronach as her young fireman has plenty of time to lean out of the cab windows to while away some time before they head off Doncaster's shed on 14 January 1962. There would be no German-style smoke deflectors for this A3 as she was withdrawn four months later. *Colour Rail*

Visitors to Doncaster Works could be forgiven for thinking they would perhaps see the unique Gresley Class W1 4-6-4 locomotive, back in action once more after an overhaul when they saw it here on 23 May 1959. However, she was posted as withdrawn within weeks and scrapped almost straightaway within the works. *Colour Rail*

The new order is replacing the old outside the sheds at Doncaster in April 1962, as the fourteen-year-old Class A1 60122 Curlew will soon be forced to give way to the three-year-old English Electric Type 4 within seven months. As another of the nation's assets is written off long before it's capital value suggested in the name of progress. *Colour Rail*

A late 1950's view of Black Five 44717 from 9E Trafford Park, seen sharing the shed yard at 41C Millhouses with a Stanier Jubilee demonstrates just how sooty these locations could be. *Colour Rail*

There is no way the rebuilt small two-road shed here at 41G Barnsley, could ever accommodate all of these locomotives present on this visit in August 1959, the shed closed just over four months later. *Colour Rail*

A small collection of ex-Great Eastern Railway types grace this view of 31C Kings Lynn shed in August 1958. The 'Heath Robinson' roof repairs only have to last until April the year after when it closed to steam, although diesels continued here until 1962. *Colour Rail*

Basking in the low sun this Gresley rebuilt Class D16/3 looks smart even in unlined black. The tablet catcher has been left extended in this view from 1956 at 32G Melton Constable. *Colour Rail*

Another well turned out Class D16/3, but this time showing the difference that lining out and a burnished smokebox ring can do for improving 62530's appearance, seen in the shed yard at 31A Cambridge on a crisp spring day during 1955. *Colour Rail*

Underneath all the grime we can see that Stratford Works had bestowed mixed traffic lining upon this humble Holden Class F5, 67202 out in the shed yard at 30A Stratford in September 1957, four months from being withdrawn. *Roy Edgar Vincent/The Transport Treasury*

Opposite: The once huge shed and works complex at Stratford yields one of Hill's Class J20 0-6-0s, 64682 on 3 October 1959. *Colour Rail*

The increasing presence of Brush Type 2s here at Stratford is apparent in both of these views, firstly with Holden's Class J17, 65507 on shed here on 8 January 1961. It was withdrawn from service just eight months later after nearly sixty-one years of service. Whereas another of his designs with this Class J69/1, 68499 waits to shunt a lame B.T.H. Type 1 back into the works building. *Photos: Gerald T. Robinson & Colour Rail*

Opposite: A second appearance for 46245 City of London on 9 June 1963, as she gleams in the morning sunlight setting back into the platforms at Kings Cross around 9 am with an inspector on the footplate. Today's run to Doncaster for the works visit will see this Stanier Pacific make a very fast run back to Kings Cross, especially on the run back down from Stoke Summit. *Colour Rail*

Many of the passengers are sporting red buttonholes, as they jostle for a chance somehow to grab a photograph for themselves before departure time here at Kings Cross on 1 May 1968. Wisely our cameraman has chosen some elevation to bring us this splendid view of the scene out towards the Deltic in the servicing shed. This was the jointly organized Alan Peglar/L.C.G.B. 40th Anniversary Non-Stop Run From Kings Cross to Edinburgh, hauled throughout on the outward run by 4472 Flying Scotsman. The return run back to London's St. Pancras was behind Class 45 Peak D97. *Colour Rail*

Staff at 34A Kings Cross have been to work again cleaning up and burnishing this Gresley Class N2/2, 69504 complete with its condensing apparatus. It was one of five locomotives used that day as it worked this second leg of the R.C.T.S sponsored London & North Kent Railtour on 21 March 1959. Its duties had been to take over from Class N7/4, 69714 at Canonbury for the run here to meet London Transport's 1938 tube stock at East Finchley where it ran around for the return run to Finsbury Park, where Class J50, 68986 would take over. *Colour Rail*

Unlike the previously described R.C.T.S. tour, their Nidd Valley Special on 19 October 1963, used this Fowler Class 4MT, 42409 from 55A Leeds Holbeck throughout. Aside from our photographer, there is just a lone spectator here at Wetherby to see its passing on this eighty-five-mile journey today.
Colour Rail

In the late-summer of 1949 when it was still just a few months old, Class A1 60127 heads south from York in its original blue livery before naming as Wilson Worsdell, which took place in October a year later. *Colour Rail*

Resplendent in garter blue, with minimal lining and red wheels the Class A4 60007 Sir Nigel Gresley was posed outside the new Rugby Testing Station for the opening ceremony in October 1948. This was only appropriate and proper as the great engineer had been the driving force to see it built. Originally envisioned as a joint LMS and LNER facility, construction was started in the late 1930s but then deferred by the war. The choice of Rugby as the location was one with access to both LMS and LNER main lines, via the WCML and the ex-Great Central. Representing the former LMS at the ceremony the same day was Duchess 46256 Sir William Stanier, F.R.S. *Colour Rail*

Take your pick for which of these two early livery schemes you prefer, whether it be the lined apple green adorning Gresley Class B17/6, 61665 Leicester City, or the flame coloured lining and lettering applied to the black painted Thompson Class B1, 61058. Standing from the taxi and parcels vehicle access point at Liverpool Street station in 1949 we can see them both to advantage. *Roy Edgar Vincent/The Transport Treasury*

Opposite: An earlier visit to the same spot in September 1948, yields one of the two streamlined Class B17s, with 61659 East Anglian in company with a duo of Thompson Class B1s in differing liveries.
Roy Edgar Vincent/The Transport Treasury

A deeper shade of blue is being worn by this Gresley Class A4, 60005 Sir Charles Newton when recorded at York in June 1950. The locomotive is also further set off with black and white lining and the new crest.
Colour Rail

Two more of Gresley's Pacifics to wear this attractive livery variant were Class A3, 60072 Sunstar visiting York's shed from Heaton in September 1949. Then a visit to the coal stage at Grantham, finds Class A4 60025 Falcon still carrying this early paint scheme on 22 June 1952.
Both: Colour Rail

Built-in November 1946, Class A2/3, 60517 Ocean Swell found itself in a lined apple green livery soon after nationalisation when seen at Newcastle Central in November 1948. A year or so later, and the more familiar lined brunswick green has been settled upon instead, for prestige locomotives, such as Class A2, 60525 A.H. Peppercorn. Although the earlier style of black livery could still be found on Class D49, 62746 The Middleton alongside, as they reside on shed at York. *Both: Colour Rail*

Opposite: Based out of 31B March, when seen at York on 14 June 1959. This Gresley Class V2, 60858 waits to head south once again with what looks like a Newcastle to Colchester service which was often worked as far as Ely by a March based Class V2. *Rail Photoprints*

The smoke is drifting from something behind the single chimney of Class A4, 60018 Sparrow Hawk as she is very much out of steam, tucked away at the back of the shed at York awaiting further repairs to her motion on 26 May 1957. *Colour Rail*

Opposite: Diesel fumes are now starting to overtake the comforting smells of coal smoke, hot oil and steam around the shed yard here at York by 3 April 1965. Notice the differing smokebox numberplate positions for these two Thompson Class B1s. *R.C.T.S. Archive*

Opposite: There seems to be little enthusiasm to keep the Puku nameplates fitted to Thompson Class B1, 61012 clean at all, as it was recorded prancing through York's centre roads in July 1961. It was based at this time out of 50B Hull Dairycoates. *Colour Rail*

A spread of Type 4 diesels are now beginning to outnumber steam locomotives stabled in the shed yards at York on 13 October 1963, as Class A4 60005 Sir Charles Newton catches our photographer's attention. *Rail Online*

Opposite: A chance to raise our spirits briefly once more with two portrait shots from an era when steam was often kept a little cleaner, with Class A1 60121 Silurian taking water, before leaving the shed to take over a northbound express in the mid-fifties. Then with a recently ex-works Class K3, 61927 also ready to head northwards from York shed in September 1959. *Both: Colour Rail*

Today's footplate crew have now turned their Class B1, 61049 since we last saw it on page 59 here at York on 3 April 1965. With a fresh charge of coal and a top-up for the tender, they will telephone the York powerbox for permission to leave the shed yard shortly, when they are satisfied all is well and have moved up to the departure signal. Note the two different styles of coal brazier, nearby. *R.C.T.S. Archive*

64 YORK 1966?

It would be nice if some of 51A Darlington's cleaners (if they still had any that is), were to set to work on this named Class V2, 60809 The Snapper, The East Yorkshire Regiment, The Duke of York's Own when seen at York on 17 August 1962. After all, it won't bite, will it? **Colour Rail**

Opposite: This is much better, as 40A Lincoln shows the way with their Class D16, 62571 all dressed up and prepared to work this enthusiast's special back to Nottingham Midland, after an interesting route out and back to visit Hull docks on 12 May 1957. The 4-4-0 worked the tour throughout. **Colour Rail**

The once-popular car-carrier service linking London with Scotland in the days before the rise of the motorways and its fall from grace, is seen near Selby in the hands of Gresley Class A4, 60021 Wild Swan around 1960. A more dramatic fall from grace befell this Ivatt Class 4MT, 43072 on 10 November 1964. While working a train of twenty-one empty wagons from Ardsley, the driver lost control at Laisterdyke and ran into Adolphus St. goods yard at an estimated speed of 50 mph. Before demolishing the buffers the crew jumped clear and the train crashed through a wall to fall 30ft here into Dryden Street below. Considered beyond economic repair was cut up in the roadway here by G.W. Butler of Laisterdyke as we see four days later. *Both: Colour Rail*

On the other hand, far better fortune with ultimate preservation awaited this Fairburn Class 4MT, 42073 within a year of this view at St. Dunstan's on 15 March 1967.
Colour Rail

COPLEY HILL 27/1/62

Some of the once extensive goods yards to be found all around the city of Leeds can be seen in the background, behind this view of Class A1, 60144 King's Courier near Copley Hill on 13 May 1961. *Colour Rail*

Opposite: The clean luxury Pullman coaches bring shame upon the external condition of Class A3, 60069 Sceptre being sent out in this state to work The Yorkshire Pullman past its home shed of 56C Copley Hill on 15 September 1960. *Colour Rail*

One of Sunderland shed's Raven Class A8s, 69852 sets back the stock from an earlier arrival here at Durham for stabling back towards the soon to closed engine shed, seen in the background to this view from 21 September 1958. *Rail Photoprints*

Opposite: We are out once again in open countryside and the market gardens around the level crossing, part of the way up Seaham bank next, to watch a very clean 65894 plod sedately up the steep incline with a short goods. This fortunate Class J27 was the chosen 'pet' for the members of the NELPG who went on to later preserve the locomotive. *Colour Rail*

Conversely, the external condition of fellow Class J27, 65817 from 52G Sunderland shed suggests some degree of hard work and thrashing recently, most likely on the steeply graded Silksworth branch, judging from the scorched away paintwork around its smokebox when seen near Ryhope Junction on 7 August 1965. *Tony Butcher*

Once again nothing too strenuous for the later to be preserved 65894 in this view, just a little gentle shunting today and another ride out into the countryside at Kirkbymoorside. *Colour Rail*

Likewise, the blood and custard colour scheme for this express stock shows up nicely behind Class V2, 60947 going well at Challoners Whin Junction on 2 June 1957. *Colour Rail*

On Eastern Metals

Its been very cold overnight on 22 December 1962, as the 'Great Freeze' starts to set in here at Bottesford on the Grantham to Nottingham line. The cold shows off the surplus of steam screaming out from the safety valves of Class B1, 61393 as they draw in with a stopper. *Colour Rail*

Opposite: Similarly, a few days later after the holidays in January 1963, things show no sign of improvement here at Oakleigh Park on the ECML as 60022 Mallard displays her prowess even in these freezing conditions with an express. *Colour Rail*

Its another freezing cold day in early 1963 at Kings Cross and the steam heating being generated from 60015 Quicksilver's boiler will be most welcomed by the passengers. *Colour Rail*

It would have been a fairly relaxed and easy turn of duty for the fireman aboard this Class N2/4, posted for pilot duties here at Peterborough on 10 September 1960. *Colour Rail*

The almost ecclesiastical architecture of Ketton and Collyweston station near Stamford reverberates the exhaust back of this passing Thompson rebuilt Class O1, 63646 on a coal working through this sleepy ex-LNWR location. *Colour Rail*

A busy scene greets us at South Lynn in 1958, as Class N7/3 69694 takes water, in the adjoining platform an Ivatt Class 4MT 'Black Pig' has charge of a Great Yarmouth to Birmingham service as some passengers seem to be giving the inspector a hard time. *Colour Rail*

Gresley's steam designs alongside brand new English Electric Deltic locomotives perhaps epitomise the early sixties scene on the ECML for many of us. In our first view we are at Peterborough with a background dominated by the power station in July 1961, as the brand new and as yet un-named D9004 pulls out to meet the arriving 60832 at the head of this Class V2 hauled semi-fast. *Colour Rail*

Opposite: Then towards the latter part of 1961, we are at the buffer stops at Kings Cross soon after D9008 has arrived. The Deltic is still almost two years away from being named as The Green Howards, as it shares the stage alongside 60028 Walter K. Whigham which is about to enter its last year of traffic along the ECML. *Colour Rail*

Opposite: Nicely presented and patiently waiting for the guard's starting whistle and green flag, 60025 Falcon stands at Kings Cross with the 18.20 to Leeds, certainly well-coaled for the journey ahead during May 1961. *Colour Rail*

Everyone goes about their business and spotters while away the time between arrivals oblivious to our cameraman taking his photograph of them and Class A1, 60118 Archibald Sturrock from 56C Copley Hill, making ready to depart back to Yorkshire during 1961. *Colour Rail*

A much busier scene at Kings Cross looking down into the locomotive yard on 20 June 1959, as Class L1 67783 waits for some further pilot work in the stub in the background. Meanwhile, 60111 Robert the Devil has a full tender setting back onto its train, just as 60021 Wild Swan backs out at the same time in search of coal after its arrival from the north. The six coaches behind 60108 Gay Crusader are unlikely to quickly deplete the coal supply in its tender on this semi-fast working at Brookmans Park on 28 February 1959. *Both: Colour Rail*

The Cathedral Church of the Blessed Virgin Mary of Lincoln dominates the skyline as one of Thompson's named Class B1s, 61009 Hartebeeste creeps into the city light engine on 8 July 1959. *Colour Rail*

Opposite: Footplate crews fill in their time between shunting work, by fastidiously cleaning their two Liverpool Street 'pet' pilots Class J69/1 68619 and Class N7/4, 69614 on 13 August 1960. *Colour Rail*

Less than a year's activity ahead remains for Hornsey's Class J50/4, 68981, with signs of modernization now encroaching all around Kings Cross on 20 June 1960. *Colour Rail*

'You had better pull your socks up young man if you want a chance to clear all of your V2s'. This is 60841 working south with coal through Grantham on 21 December 1962. *Colour Rail*

Eastern Region station colours decorate Peterborough East station in 1963, but it was served in the main by London Midland Region locomotives running in from Northampton, such as this Black Five and Class 4F. Closure to passenger traffic for the station came on 6 June 1966. *Colour Rail*

Opposite: If we include the sixteen Thompson Class B1s renumbered into the Eastern Region's Departmental series we have a total of sixty-two locomotives, seventeen of which were built by Sentinel just like Dept.38 seen at work on the seafront at Lowestoft in the mid-fifties. *Strathwood Library Collection*

Opposite: Having just hooked on to a northbound service at Grantham, the driver of Class A3, 60056 Centenary sets off with a few words of wisdom to his colleagues perhaps about Christmas on 21 December 1962. Compare the locomotive back against page 27. *Colour Rail*

Perhaps those german exhaust deflectors do make a difference after all, as this shot of fellow Class A3, 60050 Persimmon suggests, as they cross Markham Moor on a cold and misty morning in 1962. *Colour Rail*

The last of the Holden Class J17s to be built was 65589 in December 1910, she will just about make her fiftieth year, as withdrawal will not come until January the year after this shot was taken, at Mildenhall on 5 March 1960. DMUs from Cambridge took over just before closure here on 18 June 1962. *Colour Rail*

We can get this all sorted out with some jacks and large blocks of wood to get another fellow Class J17, 65558 back on her wheels properly once more, having split the points at Oulton Broad on 7 October 1958, albeit with the help of Class J15, 65478 and the Lowestoft breakdown gang. *Colour Rail*

Opposite: The Saturday morning spotters are in place at Grantham on 27 January 1962, to watch as Class B1, 61281 snakes into the station having been given the road to head for High Dyke with a rake of iron-ore empties. *Rail Photoprints*

A quick toot on the chime whistle to remind our cameraman to keep well back from 60003 Andrew K. McCosh as the Gresley Class A4 sweeps around the curves at Gainsborough in the early sixties. *Colour Rail*

At least fifteen spotters are also on hand here to watch and perhaps get in the way for the on-duty shunter at Peterborough, just as the driver of Class A1, 60132 Marmion sets back carefully onto his passenger train, after another diesel failure. *Colour Rail*

Opposite: The fireman attends to his coal for the next run back to Ongar from here at Epping, meanwhile, his driver scans back through the coaches to see if anyone has perhaps left a copy of today's newspaper behind. All under the watchful eyes of a young schoolboy on 11 October 1952. The last of these Holden designed Class F5s would linger on until the late spring of 1958. *Colour Rail*

Its all pretty leisurely here at North Woolwich on 13 June 1959, with what looks like a rake of Gresley's articulated suburban stock behind Class N7/3, 69682. At this point, 30A Stratford had another sixty of these 0-6-2Ts designed by Hill for the Great Eastern Railway on its books to call upon. *Colour Rail*

This three coach load for a Class 4MT Mogul suggests it is pretty easy to race away from Caister-on-Sea as they follow the M&GNR's line from Yarmouth Beach to Cromer along this coastal route which sadly closed in 1959.
Colour Rail

Plenty of time for conversation at Beccles today, after the arrival of an up Yarmouth extra, utilizing 61618 Wynyard Park, one of Gresley's Class B17/6 4-6-0s designed for East Anglian routes. *Colour Rail*

The Thetford to Bury St. Edmunds line had closed to passengers in 1953 but goods traffic as sparse as it often was, hung on until 27 June 1960. Three months beforehand, 31A Cambridge based Class J17, 65578 attends to the shunting at Barnham. *Colour Rail*

Much of the goods traffic within the East Anglian section of the Eastern Region was very seasonal, with some months of the year attracting good business for the railway, in between those long quiet periods. This gave a good excuse for so many closures, not just in the Beeching era but sometimes much further back. One such example was here at Haverhill where we see Class B2, 61644 Earlham Hall at the ex-Great Eastern Railway's Haverhill North on 19 October 1959. This station closed in 1967, however, the terminus station at Haverhill South saw its closure as far back as 1924. *Colour Rail*

Light engine manoeuvers within the busy confines of the final approaches to Liverpool Street station needed to be carried out swiftly and with great care, such as this one with 61616 Fallodon, another of Gresley's Class B2 locomotives. *Colour Rail*

Opposite: As a result even well into the era of diesel traction which followed, the Liverpool Street locomotive servicing point could be busy at times. In July 1959, 32A Norwich based Britannia Pacific 70034 Thomas Hardy seeks refuge here before returning home on another express. *Rail Photoprints*

Opposite: For almost thirty years Gresley's Class A4s were the pride of the fleet along the ECML, from the arrival of the first one named Silver Link in September 1935, to the dismissal of the last ones still in service during their 'Indian summer' of 1966. Among these last survivors was 60009 Union of South Africa, seen beforehand backing out of Kings Cross in the early sixties. *Colour Rail*

Steam activity around Doncaster was getting scarcer by the month as we moved into February 1967, so the opportunity to go for night exposures was becoming more important for some of those adventurous photographers of the day, in order to capture scenes such as this, of the 20.20 from Bradford which has arrived behind Black Five 45208 from 56D Mirfield. *Colour Rail*

131

Class N2/2, 69504 is caught brewing up nicely in preparation to lift a rake of empty stock away from Kings Cross in June 1960 while it was still allocated to 34B Hornsey. *Colour Rail*

Opposite: Not so much glamour today for 60103 Flying Scotsman as she rattles a fitted freight along the ECML near Markham in 1962, during her last full summer of British Railway's use. *Colour Rail*

LINCOLN 298647

She might be blowing off from her safety valves, but War Department Austerity 90428 as a bare minimum could do with a good clean up and perhaps a works visit would be a bonus when seen passing New Southgate in the early sixties. *Colour Rail*

We fear this fine-looking Gresley Class O2 will never look this good again when photographed in the lines at Doncaster on 27 May 1962, what a waste as she was withdrawn sixteen months later. *Colour Rail*

Another instance of a works visit coming just before a fall from grace also befell 60102 Sir Frederick Banbury, being withdrawn seventeen months after this stunning shot of her posed on shed at Grantham in June 1960. *Colour Rail*

Canklow shed will soon be gaining back their ex-works Austerity 90153, after this visit to Doncaster for an overhaul around 1963, this would no doubt see it through until being withdrawn from 41J Langwith Junction in February 1966. *Colour Rail*

GORTON 4-66?

8-63 DONCASTER

You would want the full operating weight of around one hundred and twenty-five tons of this Class B1 to be nicely balanced on the turntable here at Whitby, to make life as easy possible for yourself as a footplateman in May 1964. *Colour Rail*

150 Borough Gardens MPD↑
1959

20/9/58↑   153   Sunderland

Gateshead would be the final allocation for this Class V1 from September 1963 until it was taken out of traffic in November 1964. Prior to this, it had spells at Heaton, also to both Hull's Botanic Gardens and Dairycoates, finally to Thornaby before arriving here at Gateshead. In early 1965 another visit to this Tyneside shed found this Class J27 recently returned from Darlington Works with its safety valves lifting as it stands over the pits. *Both: Colour Rail*

Towards the close of steam activity in the North East, West Hartlepool's coal stage became a familiar backdrop to the work of many photographers visiting here. North Blyth's Class J27, 65811 has dropped in for its tender to be topped up with both coal and water in the early summer of 1967. Likewise, another visitor to the coal stage the year beforehand on 19 September, was Class K1, 62044 which had been a 51C Hartlepool based engine since that April, although nobody has yet fitted a new shed plate it seems. *Both: Colour Rail*

CONSETT 23.7.60

A few moments later also on 23 July 1960, 52B Heaton's Class K3, 61818 has joined 63470 on shed at Tyne Dock with its cylinder drain cocks open as she comes to a halt.
Colour Rail